Through the ART door

Easy to Follow Art Therapy Techniques

Dr. Ashima Narula

White Falcon Publishing

Through the Art Door
Ashima Narula

Published by White Falcon Publishing
Chandigarh, India

The contents of this book have been certified and timestamped
on the Gnosis blockchain as a permanent proof of existence.
Scan the QR code or visit the URL given on the back cover
to verify the blockchain certification for this book.

The views expressed in this work are solely those of the author
and do not reflect the views of the publisher, and the publisher
hereby disclaims any responsibility for them.

Requests for permission should be addressed to the publisher.

ISBN - 979-8-89222-446-8

PREFACE

Welcome to Through the Art Door, a guide that's very close to my heart. As an expressive art therapist, I've had the privilege of witnessing countless moments where people discover the profound impact that art can have on their lives. But I've also seen the hesitation—the uncertainty about what art therapy truly is, often clouded by myths and misconceptions. Many people come to their first session skeptical, unsure if this process is for them. And then, something magical happens. Slowly, they begin to open up, and the art becomes a mirror to emotions they didn't even know were buried within. The surprise, the connection, the realization that art can heal —it's always a beautiful experience to witness.

I know how overwhelming it can be to manage emotions, especially in today's fast-paced world. That's why I created this guide—to offer art therapy and creative practices to anyone seeking a deeper connection with themselves. Whether this is your first encounter with art therapy or you're looking to enrich your creative journey, my hope is that this book provides a safe, nurturing space for you to explore, reflect, and heal. Each technique is designed to be accessible, offering you simple yet meaningful ways to tap into your inner world.

So, as you open this book and step through the art door, remember that this is your space. A space to feel, to create, and to discover. May these pages guide you toward healing, growth, and a deeper understanding of yourself.

With warmth and creativity,

Dr. Ashima Narula
Founder, Therapy Palette

STEP THROUGH THE ART DOOR

Welcome to "Through the Art Door"! As you open this guide, you're stepping into a world where creativity unlocks new possibilities. This book is your key to exploring and discovering more about yourself through art.

Imagine each page as a doorway to new insights and personal growth. With every art exercise, you'll embark on a journey of self-discovery, finding new ways to express your thoughts and feelings. Remember, not every activity may resonate with you, and that's perfectly okay. Each person's creative journey is unique, and it's important to find what works best for you.

As you move through these pages, embrace each creative exploration as a chance to connect more deeply with yourself. Enjoy the process and let your artistic adventure unfold at your own pace.

The idea for this book was born during a conversation Ashima and I had about making art therapy more accessible to everyone. As mental health advocates, we realized how important it is not only for individuals but also for the unsung heroes—mental health professionals themselves. In the midst of their demanding work, they often overlook the importance of self-care, making a self-help guide like this an invaluable resource to support their well-being as well.

Our goal is to create something that professionals can use in their own self-care practice, offering them a space to pause, reflect, and recharge. I truly believe that this book is a step toward supporting both those in need of healing and those who dedicate their lives to the healing of others. Through art, we can all connect with our inner selves, no matter who we are or what role we play in the world.

Thank you for joining us on this journey of creativity, self-expression, and healing.

Warm regards,

Madhur Krishan Khosla
Co-Founder, Therapy Palette

ACKNOWLEDGMENT

This book would not have been possible without the support and contributions of incredible individuals.

First and foremost, I want to express my deepest gratitude to my colleague and shadow art therapist, Ms. Anshika Rana. Her creativity, dedication, and insightful contributions have shaped this book in ways words cannot express. From brainstorming to bringing the vision to life, she has been an integral part of this journey. She approached each task with passion, offering insights and ideas that breathed life into the pages. Thank you for your belief in this project and for standing by me every step of the way.

I am deeply grateful to my incredible team at Therapy Palette. I would like to extend my deepest gratitude to Ankita—her creative vision and tireless efforts in managing our social media presence have been instrumental in spreading the word about our work and this book.

To Madhur, my co-founder and partner—his insightful ideas and commitment to making art therapy accessible have shaped not only this book but the very foundation of Therapy Palette.

To my family and friends, your unwavering love and support have been the foundation that keeps me grounded. Your belief in me, especially during moments of doubt, has been my strength. Whether it was through a kind word, a listening ear, or simply being present, you've made this journey lighter and filled it with warmth. Your presence in my life has been a true gift, and I am forever grateful. I extend my heartfelt thanks to my mentors and guides; their teachings have profoundly shaped my understanding and approach. Their insights have been a cornerstone of my professional growth, and I am sincerely appreciative of their enduring support and guidance.

hello Creative Souls,

I'm a practicing psychologist and expressive art therapist & educator. I am a founder of Therapy Palette: Mental Health Clinic & Art Therapy Studio, living in Delhi, India. As an expressive art therapist, with PhD in psychology, I bring a wealth of knowledge and experience to the table. My academic background equips me to understand the intricacies of the human mind. I am also a registered Creative Dance Movement Therapist with UNESCO-CID, which adds a unique dimension to my therapeutic approach.

Dr. Ashima Narula

I am a proud professional member of the International Expressive Arts Therapy Association (IEATA), signifying my dedication to ethical and effective therapeutic practices. With this blend of academic excellence, creative movement therapy expertise, and a commitment to ongoing growth, I love to guide individuals toward self-discovery, healing, and personal growth. Not only I am dedicated to individual well-being, but I have also had the privilege of sharing my expertise by training students in expressive art therapy.

Over the years, I've had the privilege of walking alongside individuals in their most vulnerable moments, offering a safe space for expression and connection. In these moments, I've witnessed how creativity can gently open doors to parts of ourselves we didn't even know were there, allowing for deep reflection and transformation. It's a humbling experience to be trusted with such personal stories, and I am continually inspired by the resilience and courage people show in their healing journey.

CONTENT

WHAT YOU'LL FIND INSIDE

This book is not just a guide; it's an invitation to embark on a journey of self-discovery and healing through art. Within these pages, you'll find 30 art techniques, each one like a key, unlocking doors to deeper understanding. Just as a river flows, carrying with it the story of the land it passes, so too will these activities help you navigate your inner landscape—gently uncovering what's beneath the surface.

This book is a melody of various art forms—visual arts, digital art, creative writing, nature-inspired art, music, and movement techniques. Each approach is designed to help you express your emotions and experiences in ways that feel natural and empowering. Whether you're sculpting with clay, writing poetic reflections, or dancing like the wind, these activities offer endless opportunities for play, growth, and healing.

Whether you're a therapist eager to expand your toolkit or an individual looking to reconnect with your creative spirit, this book offers a map to explore uncharted territory. The art you create will become a mirror, reflecting parts of yourself you may not have noticed before. With each technique, you'll be invited to draw, write, move, and paint your emotions, creating visual stories that words alone may not express.

This is not about creating "masterpieces" but about embracing the process, like planting seeds in the soil of your soul. Some seeds will grow into beautiful blooms, while others may need more time to take root. Each mark on the page, each sculpture or collage, represents a step forward, an exploration of who you are and who you are becoming.

Through the activities and reflective prompts, you'll find space to release, play, and express your truest self. Like a lighthouse guiding ships to shore, this book will help you navigate the waves of your emotions, providing tools to not only express but to heal.

HOW TO FULLY ENGAGE WITH THIS GUIDE

This book invites you to embark on a journey of self-discovery, creativity, and healing. To help you fully engage with the process, here are a few ways to create the most enriching experience:

Cultivate Your Safe Creative Space

Before diving into the techniques, take a moment to cultivate a space where you feel comfortable and open. Whether it's a cozy corner of your home, a quiet studio, or a calming outdoor setting, surround yourself with objects or materials that bring you peace. Let this be a safe and nurturing environment where your creativity can flow freely.

Set an Intention

Every session begins with intention. Whether your goal is emotional release, reflection, or simply a moment of quiet, set a purpose for each activity. By aligning your heart with your hands, you invite deeper meaning into your creative process.

Welcome the Unknown

There is no right or wrong in art—it's all about exploration. Allow yourself to experiment, to try new techniques, and to make mistakes. Often, it's in the unexpected turns where the most profound insights emerge. Approach each activity with a sense of play and curiosity.

HOW TO FULLY ENGAGE WITH THIS GUIDE

Honor Your Journey with Compassion

As you navigate through these techniques, be gentle with yourself. Creativity, like healing, is a process. You may uncover emotions or memories that are tender or challenging. Hold space for them with kindness. Practice self-compassion and let go of judgment—your art is a reflection of your journey, not a product to perfect.

Foster a Supportive Environment

Whether you're working alone or with others, surround yourself with positivity. If you're facilitating these techniques in a group setting, encourage an atmosphere of openness and respect. If you're exploring this book solo, consider journaling or sharing your experience with a trusted friend or therapist.

Seek Support When Needed

If the process becomes overwhelming or you encounter difficult emotions, don't hesitate to seek support. Whether from a therapist, mentor, or a loved one, asking for help is a courageous step toward healing. Art has the power to reveal, but you never have to navigate those revelations alone.

A GENTLE REMINDER

While I am a practicing psychologist and expressive arts therapist, the information and techniques provided in this book do not constitute psychological or mental health advice, nor do they establish any form of therapist-client relationship. The content within is intended solely for educational and informational purposes and is not a substitute for professional therapy or art therapy sessions. This guide is created to help you explore self-expression, self-reflection, stress relief, and personal growth through art. Using these techniques with clients does not qualify you to call yourself an art therapist.

Each prompt in this guide has been thoughtfully designed to inspire self-reflection, creativity, and a deeper connection with oneself. Many prompts have been created by Dr. Ashima, while some are rooted in established art therapy theories, research, and practices. Grateful acknowledgment to all the pioneers who laid the foundation for this work!

This book should not be used in place of individualized therapeutic support. Readers are encouraged to seek guidance from a qualified mental health professional, particularly before making any medical or psychological decisions. Although every effort has been made to ensure the accuracy of the information provided, this book is not intended to replace professional advice tailored to your specific needs and circumstances.

Whether you're new to art or have years of experience, these prompts are open to everyone and don't require any artistic background. However, always be mindful of your emotional limits. If your art-making stirs deep emotions, make sure you have the right support, whether it's family, friends, or a therapist to help guide you.

As an art therapist, I've seen firsthand the incredible impact that art can have on a person's life. Through my own experiences and those of my clients, I've witnessed art become a powerful tool for self-expression, healing, and personal growth. My hope is that this guide will inspire you to explore your creativity, connect with your inner self, and discover the transformative power of art in enhancing your well-being. The journey with art is limitless, and there is always more to explore.

This is a guide featuring therapeutic art prompts created by an art therapist, but it is not a form of art therapy.
What does this mean?

ART THERAPY VS. THERAPEUTIC ART: A SIMPLE GUIDE

Imagine two paths through a forest—both filled with creativity and self-expression, but each leading to a different place. One path is more structured and guided, while the other allows you to wander and explore freely.

Art Therapy

Art therapy is like walking through a well-planned garden. Every flower, tree, and path has been carefully chosen with a purpose. In this garden, you have a guide—an art therapist—who helps you use art to heal emotional wounds and support your mental health. The art you create here is a tool to express feelings that might be too difficult to put into words. Art therapy is guided by a trained professional and uses specific techniques to promote healing and personal growth.

Therapeutic Art

Therapeutic art, on the other hand, is more like walking through a wild, open meadow. There are no set paths, and you're free to explore as you like, picking wildflowers along the way. It's about the simple joy of creating, without worrying about achieving a specific goal. Therapeutic art may not involve a therapist, but it still provides emotional release, comfort, and moments of reflection. It helps you connect with yourself in a personal and creative way, without the formal structure of art therapy.

IT'S NOT ABOUT THE FINAL PIECE, IT'S ABOUT THE JOURNEY YOU TAKE WHILE CREATING.

LET'S GET STARTED

Before you dive in, here's a quick note: there's no need to rush out and buy loads of art supplies! Begin with what you have and what feels right for you. Start simple, start comfortable!

HERE ARE THE ESSENTIAL SUPPLIES THAT KEEP MY CREATIVITY FLOWING!

- Markers
- Sketch pens (thick or thin)
- Brush pens
- Glitter pens
- Soft pastels
- Oil pastels
- Crayons

RESISTIVE MEDIA

FLUID MEDIA

- Watercolor paints
- Acrylic paints
- Gouache paints
- Paint brushes (round or flat)
- Paper towel
- Water bowl

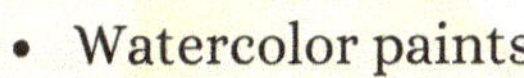
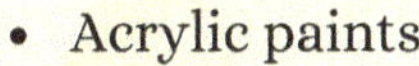

- Paper (different sizes)
- Scissors
- Glue
- Canvas
- Tape

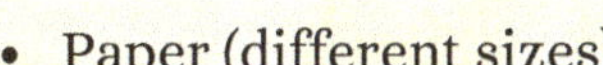
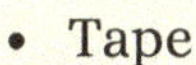

BASIC SUPPLY

LET'S GET STARTED

- Beads, stones, pebbles
- Fabric, yarn string
- Glitter
- Modeling clay

EMBELLISHMENTS

- Collage kit
- Stickers
- Magazines or Newspaper
- Scrapbook paper

MIXED MEDIA

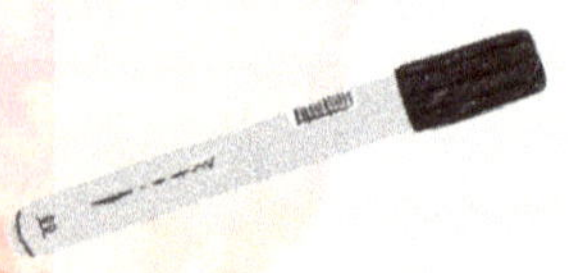

AROUND THE HOUSE

- Shoebox or courier box
- Chocolate wrappers
- Ribbons or threads
- Buttons
- From the kitchen
- Sticks
- Nature elements from garden

You can create impactful art with just a pencil and paper. However, having a variety of supplies on hand can make it easier to express yourself more fully and enjoy the process of play and exploration!

HOW TO USE THIS BOOK

This book is designed to be a practical guide for therapists, facilitators, and individuals interested in the healing power of art. Whether you're a seasoned professional or new to therapeutic art practices, the following instructions will help you make the most of each technique presented.

Understanding the layout

Each of the 30 techniques follows a simple, structured format:

- **Technique Name**

Every technique begins with a clear title, giving you insight into the theme or approach of the activity.

- **Materials Required**

This section lists all the necessary supplies for the activity. From simple tools like pencils and paper to more specialized items like paints or clay, you'll know exactly what you need to get started. Feel free to substitute materials based on availability or participant preferences.

- **Instructions**

Here, you'll find a step-by-step guide to facilitating or performing the activity. These instructions are crafted to be flexible, allowing you to adapt them for personal reflection or any individual setting.

- **Reflection Questions**

After completing each activity, a set of reflection questions invites you to explore your emotions, thoughts, and insights. These open-ended prompts encourage deeper understanding and connection to the artwork created, fostering meaningful discussions or personal introspection.

Remember, you can move through the book at your own pace. Choose an activity that resonates with your current emotions or challenges, and allow yourself the freedom to express without judgment. Use the reflection questions to journal about your experience, noting any insights or shifts in perspective that arise from the creative process.

> **"I FOUND I COULD SAY THINGS WITH COLOUR AND SHAPES THAT I COULDN'T SAY ANY OTHER WAY – THINGS I HAD NO WORDS FOR."**
> **– GEORGIA O'KEEFE**

A Flexible Guide

While each technique has been carefully designed, remember that art is inherently flexible. There are no rigid rules—this book is a starting point for you to adapt, expand, and explore in ways that feel authentic. The process of making art can be transformative, so allow yourself and your clients or participants the freedom to engage deeply with each activity.

INTERPRETING YOUR ART

A common misunderstanding about art therapy is that an art therapist interprets your artwork. In reality, interpreting your art is a personal journey of exploration and reflection, not about uncovering hidden meanings dictated by someone else.

As you complete the activities and reflect on your experiences, you may find that you gain valuable insights into your emotions and thoughts. Art-making serves as a mirror for your feelings and helps you connect with your inner self. By consistently engaging with your creativity and trusting your artistic instincts, you open the door to deeper self-discovery.

Remember, it's okay if your art doesn't turn out as planned or if you don't see a deeper meaning right away. Allow yourself to make mistakes and see where the creative process takes you.

WHY YOU SHOULD TRY THERAPEUTIC ART TECHNIQUES?

Think of art practice as tending to a beautiful garden inside you. Each time you create, it's like planting a seed in this garden. As you continue to nurture and care for these seeds through your art, you help your inner garden grow and blossom.

Art therapy helps you explore your feelings and thoughts, just like a gardener discovers new plants and flowers in their garden. With each art activity, you're giving attention to different parts of yourself, allowing new insights and emotions to surface. Think of art practice as tending to a beautiful garden inside you.

Each time you create, it's like planting a seed in this garden. As you continue nurturing and caring for these seeds through your art, you help your inner garden grow and blossom.

By practicing art therapy, you're tending to your emotional garden, helping it flourish and become more vibrant. Each creative effort adds to the growth and beauty of your inner world, making it a place of discovery and healing.

WISHING YOU INSPIRATION AND GROWTH ON THIS CREATIVE PATH. LET'S DIVE IN AND SEE WHERE IT TAKES YOU!

INTENTION CARD

Material Required

- Cardstock
- Markers, pens, or colored pencils
- Stickers, washi tape, or decorative elements
- Glue or double-sided tape, Scissors
- Magazines or printed images (optional)
- Personal photos (optional)

Instructions

Begin by setting an intention for your self-care practice. Reflect on what you need for your well-being right now. Take a piece of cardstock and start creating your intention card. Use markers, pens, or colored pencils to design the card.

Let your creativity flow and incorporate elements that resonate with your chosen intention. Add decorative elements like stickers, washi tape, or images that reflect your intention.

You can also include personal photos or images that are meaningful to you. Review your card and make any final adjustments to ensure it accurately represents your intention and is visually appealing to you.

Visualize how this card will support you in your self-care journey and how it can serve as a reminder of your commitment to your well-being.

Reflections

While observing your work, take a moment to reflect on these questions—feel free to journal your thoughts, if it resonates with you.

- Give a title to your intention card.
- How does the process of creating this card make you feel about your self-care journey?
- What specific emotions or thoughts does your card evoke when you look at it?
- How can you integrate the intention of your card into your daily routine?

PLAYFUL PASTELS

Material Required

- Oil pastels/ soft pastels/ soft crayons
- Sheet (any size)

Instructions

Find a comfortable space for yourself, gather the art mediums (oil pastels/soft pastels or crayons), and keep them in front of you. You can also play soft music in the background (hand pan, soft instrumental, hang drum). Select any art medium of your choice.

Pause for a moment and consider which colors evoke feelings of relaxation and calm for you. Choose the ones that resonate most with that sense of peace. Pick the first color and scribble randomly on the piece of paper. Breathe slowly and have slow moments. Allow your hand to go with the flow.

Notice the sensations of the color flowing onto the paper. You can also simultaneously switch colors. When you feel you are done, step back and observe your work.

Reflections

While observing your work, take a moment to reflect on these questions—feel free to journal your thoughts, if it resonates with you.

- What color did you choose and why do you find them calming?
- What are the thoughts and feelings that emerged during the process?
- Were there any surprises that came up for you? How did it feel to slow down?

COLORFUL SPECTRUM OF SELF

Material Required

- Photo of Yourself
- Photo editing Apps (e.g., Snapseed, Adobe Lightroom, PicsArt, Colorscape)
- Markers, Crayons, Colored pencils (Optional)

Instructions

Choose a photo of yourself that you like. Use suggested photo editing software to make your photo black and white. Next, use the same software to add colors directly onto the photo, focusing on colors that you feel express your personality, mood, or the version of yourself you want to showcase. Don't worry about making it perfect—let the colors flow intuitively.

Alternatively, you can print the photo and use markers or colored pencils to add color by hand. Consider which aspects of the photo you'd like to highlight with color: Is it the background? The details of your clothing? Or maybe you want to change the entire color scheme to something bold and vibrant, or serene or peaceful.

Feel free to get creative—add patterns, shapes, or even symbols that speak to who you are. Let the process of adding color be your own unique expression of self.

Reflections

While observing your work, take a moment to reflect on these questions—feel free to journal your thoughts, if it resonates with you.

- How did it feel to see your portrait differently?
- What emotions or thoughts does your colored photo evoke?
- Does the process change the way you perceive yourself?
- What was the most surprising part of the process?

DUMPING THOUGHTS

Material Required

- Notebook or Journal
- Pen or pencil

Instructions

Find a comfortable space and gather your notebook and pen. Choose one of the given prompts. Set your timer for 20 minutes. Begin writing continuously without lifting your pen. Allow your thoughts to flow without overthinking them. If you are stuck, repeat the last word or sentence until a new thought comes to mind. Remember, it's okay if your writing seems disjointed or if you change topics. The focus is on expression. After 20 minutes, reflect on your experience.

Prompts
"I feel…."
"I want…"

Reflections

While observing your work, take a moment to reflect on these questions—feel free to journal your thoughts, if it resonates with you.

- How did it feel to write continuously without stopping?
- Were there any moments where you felt stuck during writing?
- Did any surprising thoughts or feelings emerge for you during the process?
- Were there any insights for you during the process?
- How do you feel after the process?

SLOW DIGITAL SNAPS

Material Required

- A camera or a smartphone
- A photo editing app or software (e.g., Canva, InShot, Adobe Spark, or any collage-making app)

Instructions

Begin your day by slowing down, and taking in your surroundings. Notice the details and snap photos of everything that inspires you. Look for anything that brings you a sense of joy or peace. This could be a flower, a unique building, a smiling person, or even the way the light filters through the trees.

Slow down, practice nothing, and experience joy in simple moments. Name what you appreciate. Afterward, create a digital collage using a phone editing app, or you can also create a printed photo collage from the images. Take some time to reflect on your collage and the slowness of your experience.

Reflections

While observing your work, take a moment to reflect on these questions—feel free to journal your thoughts, if it resonates with you.

- Did anything surprise you?
- What would be the title of your collage?
- When you name small moments or simple joys, how does this change your mood?
- How did creating the digital collage help you reflect on your experience?
- How can you incorporate the practice of finding joy in simple moments into your daily life?

RIP AND REBUILD

Material Required

- A piece of paper (choose any color, texture, or pattern that resonates with you)
- Additional colored or patterned paper (optional)
- Glue stick or adhesive
- Markers, colored pencils, or pens
- Stickers, symbols, or small decorative elements (optional)
- A blank sheet of paper or a sketchbook to assemble your creation

Instructions

Find a quiet, comfortable space where you feel at ease. Choose a piece of paper—it could be colored, textured, or plain—and begin tearing it into pieces. You can tear large chunks or tiny fragments, allowing your emotions and instincts to guide you in the process. There's no right or wrong way to do this, so give yourself permission to be free in your approach. When you feel ready, pause and take a moment to observe the pile of torn pieces in front of you. Reflect on what these scraps might represent for you. When you're ready, use the pieces to create something entirely new, arranging them in a way that feels meaningful to you. Feel free to enhance your creation with drawings, symbols, or even stickers, letting your inner world unfold through this process.

Reflections

While observing your work, take a moment to reflect on these questions—feel free to journal your thoughts, if it resonates with you.

- How did it feel to tear the paper?
- Did you notice any resistance or ease in this creative process?
- What does that say about how you approach change or uncertainty?
- How did it feel to tear something and then rebuild it?
- What thoughts or feelings emerged when you added additional elements like drawings, symbols, or stickers?

SENSORY SCRIBBLES

Material Required

- Soft Pastels/Chalk Pastels or Oil pastels
- Black Markers
- Pen
- Journal/Notebook

Template

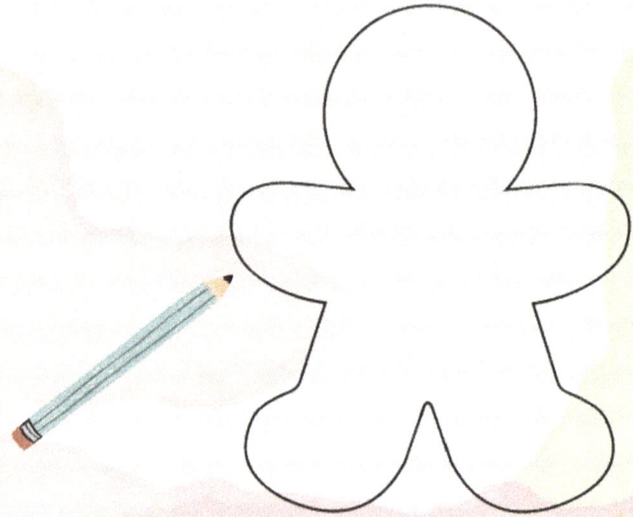

Instructions

Draw the provided body shape template in your notebook. Once you've sketched it, take a few deep, calming breaths and focus on the sensations in your body.

Using soft pastels or oil pastels, begin to scribble within the template, starting at the head and working your way down. Let your breathing guide your hand—matching the rhythm of your inhales and exhales with the movement of your scribbling. Feel free to use different colors as you move through each part of the body.

After you've filled in the body outline, turn the page and reflect on the sensations you felt while scribbling. Write down any physical or emotional feelings you experienced in each part, starting from your head and working your way down to your feet.

Reflections

While observing your work, take a moment to reflect on these questions—feel free to journal your thoughts, if it resonates with you.

- How does it feel to express physical sensations visually?
- How do you feel now compared to before you started the activity?
- Were there any areas of your body that felt more intense or different from others? Why do you think that is?
- What do you need to give your body right now?
- Do you feel any different after this process, and How?

CLAY PLAY

Material Required

- Air-drying clay or molding clay
- A bowl of water
- Paper towels
- Optional: Paints and Brushes

Instructions

Begin by taking a piece of clay and holding it in your hands. Take a moment to appreciate its texture and temperature, noticing how it feels against your skin.

Dip your fingers into a bowl of water and sprinkle some onto the clay to help soften it. Start working with the clay by pushing, pressing, and rolling it with your fingers, allowing your movements to flow naturally. As you continue, feel free to dip your fingers in the water as needed to maintain the desired consistency.

Focus on the sensations you experience as you manipulate the clay, observing how it changes and becomes softer in your hands. Once you feel connected to the material, use the softened clay to create a shape or figure that embodies your emotions and feelings during this process. After you finish your creation, let it dry completely. If you wish, you can paint it later to add an extra layer of expression. Finally, give a name to your clay work that reflects its meaning or significance to you.

Reflections

While observing your work, take a moment to reflect on these questions—feel free to journal your thoughts, if it resonates with you.

- What emotions or thoughts came up for you while playing with the clay?
- Were there any changes in your emotions from the beginning to the end of the process?
- What sensations did you feel in your hands and your body as you worked with the clay?

RHYTHMIC WORDS

Material Required

- A4 size sheet (white or colored)
- Pencils and Pens
- Colored markers, Colored pens
- Stickers, glitter, or other craft medium (optional)

Instructions

Start by taking a sheet of paper and a pen. Write your name in large, bubble letters in the center of the page. Once you've done that, take a moment to reflect on who you are.

Consider the various aspects of yourself—your hobbies, interests, relationships, personality traits, and what makes you uniquely "YOU." Surround your name with different symbols, patterns, and words that represent these qualities.

Feel free to use colored markers, stickers, and glitter to embellish each letter, making it as detailed and vibrant as you wish. Take your time and think about why you chose each element; reflect on what each pattern, symbol, or word represents and how it contributes to your sense of self.

Reflections

While observing your work, take a moment to reflect on these questions—feel free to journal your thoughts, if it resonates with you.

- What symbols and words do you use to represent yourself?
- Did you discover anything new about yourself during the process?
- Does this artwork feel like it includes all parts of you? If not, what parts of you are not there?
- Were there any difficulties that came up for you during the process?

NATURE'S MELODY

Material Required

- A4 size white sheet
- Headphones
- Paints, brushes
- Markers
- Crayons

Instructions

Visit any natural setting, such as a park or a garden. Find a comfortable spot to sit and ensure you have all the art mediums and a pair of headphones. Put your headphones on and play your favorite music.

Close your eyes, take a few deep breaths, and immerse yourself in the music. When you open your eyes, create art inspired by your experience of listening to that music while making art.

Allow the rhythm, melody, and emotions of the music to inspire your choice of colors, shapes, and lines. After you've finished, sit with yourself and reflect on your artwork.

Reflections

While observing your work, take a moment to reflect on these questions—feel free to journal your thoughts, if it resonates with you.

- Are there any surprises or elements that stand out?
- How did listening to music influence your creative process?
- How did it make you feel?
- Was there a particular moment in the music that felt especially inspiring or transformative for your artwork?
- What would be the title of your artwork?

THE FIRST CHAPTER

Material Required

- Journal or notebook
- Pen or pencil
- Optional: Laptop or tablet for digital writing

Instructions

Imagine that you are about to write a book about your life. This book is your autobiography, and you are the author of your story. How would you like the first chapter to be? What would be the theme and plot of this chapter? What significant events, experiences, or qualities do you want to highlight? What message do you wish to tell your readers? Why is this story important to tell? Start writing your first chapter. This chapter is an introduction to you. There are no right or wrong answers; this is your story to tell in your own words. Consider whether you would like to continue writing further chapters. If so, add more chapters to your autobiography. What more aspects of your life and story would you like to share? What more would you like to include in future chapters?

As you write this first chapter, allow yourself to pour your heart out onto the page. Share your joys, struggles, and the lessons learned along the way.

Reflections

While observing your work, take a moment to reflect on these questions—feel free to journal your thoughts if, it resonates with you.

- How did it feel to write the first chapter of your autobiography? Were there any surprises or new insights about yourself?
- Did you find it easy or challenging to write about your story and what to include in the chapter?
- Do you feel inspired to continue writing more chapters? What other stories or experiences would you like to explore?
- What emotions came for you while writing your story?

WALK IN CLOUDS

Material Required

- Pencil colors
- Oil Pastels
- Crayons
- Markers

Instructions

Find a comfortable space for yourself. Begin by closing your eyes or looking downwards. Take a few deep breaths. Reflect on how you are feeling right now and what is one emotion you are experiencing constantly. It could be happiness, anger, sadness, excitement, or other emotions. With that emotion in your mind, slowly open your eyes, grab your art medium, and start to scribble on the paper.

Let your emotion guide the movements of your hands. Use different lines, shapes, patterns, and colors. Focus on expressing your "emotion" rather than the outcome. Spend 10-15 minutes on this process. Once you feel you are done, take a pause and reflect on the process.

Reflections

While observing your work, take a moment to reflect on these questions—feel free to journal your thoughts, if it resonates with you.

- What was the emotion you felt?
- How did it feel to express your emotion onto the paper?
- What were the thoughts and feelings that emerged during the process?
- Do you think this process helped you understand or process your emotions, and How?
- Did you notice any changes in your feelings after the activity?

LIFE IN PICTURES

Material Required

- A3 or A4 size white sheet or Canvas
- Magazines, newspapers, old books, printed photos
- Scissors
- Glue sticks
- Markers, colored pencils, crayons
- Stickers, Washi tapes, and craft media

Instructions

Use magazines, newspapers, old books, cut-out images, words, and phrases that resonate with you or reflect elements of yourself. It could be about your favorite places, favorite things, or your personality. Lay your images on the sheet and create a collage out of them.

You can also use different arrangements and glue them onto the sheet. Draw, write, or add details to your collage with markers, colored pencils, or crayons. You can also use stickers, washi tape, and other craft media to add elements to your collage.

Reflections

While observing your work, take a moment to reflect on these questions—feel free to journal your thoughts, if it resonates with you.

- Was there anything surprising that came up for you?
- Do you feel something is missing in your collage?
- Is there anything that you would like to change or add in the future?
- How do you feel after reflecting on who you are?

NARRATIVES BY NATURE

Material Required

- Step into Nature (A Garden or a park)
- A small paper bag
- Journal
- Pen or pencil

Instructions

Visit any garden or park near you. Take a walk in nature and pay attention to your surroundings. Notice trees, flowers, birds, and other natural elements that surround you. As you walk, look for items that you connect with and collect them in the paper bag. It could be leaves, stones, flowers, sticks, feathers, or any other natural elements. Remember to be respectful of nature and avoid plucking anything. After that, find a flat surface and create an arrangement that you find pleasing. You can try different patterns and arrangements. Take a moment to observe your creation; sit back with your journal and reflect on the experience using reflection questions.

Reflections

While observing your work, take a moment to reflect on these questions—feel free to journal your thoughts, if it resonates with you.

- What were the items that you collected and why?
- What were the thoughts that came up while walking in nature?
- If you could give your creation a title, what would it be?
- Were there any difficulties or surprises that came up for you?
- Do you think engaging in this process makes you mindful and present about your surroundings?

IMAGINARY BEING

Material Required

- Air-dry clay/ polymer clay or modeling clay
- Clay modeling tools (optional)- Our hands work as best tool
- Craft medium (e.g., beads, eyes feathers, glitter)
- Journal/Notebook
- Pen

Instructions

Begin by closing your eyes and taking a few deep breaths. Visualize a creature that symbolizes your companion. Think about its shape, size, and characteristics.

What does it look like? How does it move? Which textures does it have? Using clay, bring your imaginary creature to life. As you do so, consider your creature's superpowers, which can help you handle any kind of distress or discomfort. These could be metaphorical powers like "Calm Waves" to wash away worries or other abilities. Sculpt features or symbols that represent these powers. Add more details to your creature. Take a moment to observe your creature and reflect on it using the provided questions in your journals.

Reflections

While observing your work, take a moment to reflect on these questions —feel free to journal your thoughts, if it resonates with you.

- How does this creature feel?
- Does this creature have similar or different desires, needs, or feelings than you?
- Is there anything this creature needs right now?
- What is the name of this creature and what powers this creature has?
- Would you like to say anything to this creature?

POCKET TALE

Material Required

- Pencil or pen
- White sheets of paper

Instructions

Write a story about something that happened to you, write only in five sentences. Now, write the same story in two sentences. Narrow it down further to one sentence. Finally, tell this story in three words. Write those three words at the top of a small piece of paper, then draw an image that represents the three words. Reflect on the process of writing your story and how you feel while writing it.

Reflections

While observing your work, take a moment to reflect on these questions—feel free to journal your thoughts, if it resonates with you.

- What did you notice when you got to know the essence of your story?
- Was it difficult to limit your words?
- How does expressing yourself with limited words feel different from writing a long story?
- Was this process helpful for you in any way and How?

BLACKOUT RHYTHMS

Material Required

- Blank sheets
- A printed copy of a song or poem/ page from a book you connect with
- Highlighters
- Black markers or pens
- Colored Pens

Instructions

Start by printing out the lyrics of a song, a poem, or a passage from a novel that resonates with you. Read through the text carefully and highlight the words or phrases that speak to you, whether they evoke strong emotions, memories, or thoughts. Once you've highlighted these significant words, use a black marker or pen to blackout the remaining text that you didn't choose.

Take your time with this process, being mindful of the meaning behind each highlighted word. Next, take a blank sheet of paper and write down all the words you've highlighted.

Use these words to create your own poem or song. After crafting your piece, take a moment to reflect on what your new creation means to you.

Reflections

While observing your work, take a moment to reflect on these questions —feel free to journal your thoughts, if it resonates with you.

- How do you feel after this process?
- Does your poem express something you are feeling?
- What would be the title of your new song/poem?
- Was there any meaning or insight that came up for you during the process?

PETALS AND PRICKLES

Material Required

- Nature elements (flowers and leaves)
- Paper or canvas
- Glue
- Scissors
- Markers, colored pencils, crayons, paints
- Magazines or printed images (optional)

Instructions

Gather natural elements and ensure you do not harm the environment. Place the natural elements and art mediums in front of you. Take a moment to think about your day. Identify the positive parts and the difficult parts of your day. Divide the paper into two sections

Choose natural elements, images, or words that symbolize the positive part of your day. Arrange them on the page however you like. Similarly, choose elements that symbolize the difficult part of your day. Arrange them on the paper as well. Once you have both sides represented, take a moment to observe your creation. Observe how the two components of your day coexist on paper. You can add words, drawings, and phrases to express your emotions more clearly.

Reflections

While observing your work, take a moment to reflect on these questions—feel free to journal your thoughts, if it resonates with you.

- Looking at your artwork, what do you notice?
- What do you appreciate now?
- Did combining both aspects on paper give you any new insights about your day?
- What were the emotions that came up for you during this activity?
- Is there something these moments can teach you?

MY PLANET

Material Required

- Paper (craft paper, cardboard, glitter sheets, etc.)
- Paints (acrylic, watercolor, etc.) and Brushes
- Markers and Colored Pens
- Craft supplies (foil, wool, fabric, buttons, beads, glitter, etc.)
- Glue and Tape, Scissors
- Additional craft materials as desired

Instructions

Imagine you have a superpower to create your planet. How would your planet look? Before you begin, take a moment to think about how you want your planet to feel. What emotions do you want it to evoke? Consider the colors, textures, and unique features that will make your planet truly yours. Start by selecting a piece of paper or cardboard as the base for your planet. Visualize the shape and size you'd like to create—will it be circular, oval, or perhaps something entirely unique? Use paints to lay down the base colors that reflect the mood and essence of your planet.

Next, think about the textures and details that will bring your planet to life. Use craft materials like foil for metallic surfaces, wool for softness, fabric for different textures, and buttons for added character. Consider what features your planet will have—oceans, forests, mountains, or anything that resonates with your imagination.

Reflect on the elements that will exist on your planet. Will there be water, oxygen, nature, or something entirely different? Envision the inhabitants of your planet—are there humans, animals, or fantastical creatures? Use the materials at hand to represent these components.

Once you've crafted your planet, take a moment to name it and reflect on the creative process. What did you learn about yourself while designing this unique world?

Reflections

While observing your work, take a moment to reflect on these questions—feel free to journal your thoughts, if it resonates with you.

- How did you feel while creating your planet?
- What features of your planet are most important to you, and why?
- How does your planet represent your ideal world or a place of comfort?
- What would it be if you could take one thing from this planet for your daily life?
- If you could invite someone to visit your planet, who would it be and why?

CLOSER AND BEYOND

Material Required

- A large piece of paper
- Scissors and Glue
- Magazines, newspapers, or printed images
- A photograph of yourself
- Markers or pens

Instructions

Cut out words and images from magazines, newspapers, and other printed media. Choose ones that reflect your achievements and aspects of your personality, and those that describe your goals and qualities you want to embody. Write your name and glue a photo in the center of the sheet. Glue the words and images that represent things you have already achieved or that reflect your current personality closer to your photo. Glue the words and images that symbolize your goals or the qualities you wish to develop farther away from your photo. The distance should represent how far you feel you are from achieving them. Add color, and drawings to elevate these ideas. After you've completed your collage, take some time to reflect on your achievements and what you aspire to.

Reflections

While observing your work, take a moment to reflect on these questions—feel free to journal your thoughts, if it resonates with you.

- Did you see something about yourself in a new way?
- What aspects of "who you are" do you value the most?
- How could you take a small step toward bringing the "farther" words closer today?
- How does your collage make you feel about your journey of growth?

COLORS IN MOTION

Material Required

- A3 or A4 size white sheet
- Acrylic paints or watercolor paints
- Paintbrushes
- Mixing palette
- Water cups
- Paper towel

Instructions

Find a quiet and comfortable space for you where you can move freely. Begin by playing soft instrumental music in the background. Let your body move freely on the music. You can close your eyes if you feel like it. Allow your body to flow with the rhythm of music, explore the space, and explore different movements. Remember, there's no right and wrong way to do this. After 5-10 minutes, come back and sit in front of your sheet and art mediums. Imagine what these movements might look like if you translate them into an artwork. Were they flowing or sharp? Long or Short?

Which colors would describe them? Pick your paintbrushes and translate your movements into a painting. Use different patterns and brushstrokes to represent varied emotions and sensations of the experience. Once you complete, take a moment to reflect on the experience.

Reflections

While observing your work, take a moment to reflect on these questions—feel free to journal your thoughts, if it resonates with you.

- How did moving your body and going with the flow make you feel?
- Did any emotions come up during the process?
- Was it easier for you to translate your movements onto the piece of paper?
- How would you describe your feelings after the process?

SAFE SPACE CIRCLE

Material Required

- Large Sheet of Paper
- Markers, Crayons, Oil pastels, Soft pastels
- Watercolor and paintbrushes
- Water bowl and paper towel
- Various craft mediums (stickers, tape, glitter, etc.)

Instructions

On your large sheet of paper, start by drawing a big bubble that symbolizes your boundaries. Inside the bubble, represent yourself in whatever way feels right—this could be a simple stick figure, a heart, or a more intricate design.

Use colors, stickers, or cut-out images that resonate with you. Next, think about the people, pets, or objects you want to include in your bubble.

Illustrate them inside with you. Now, consider who or what you'd like to keep outside your bubble. Draw these elements outside the boundary. Feel free to add any extra details that make this bubble a true reflection of your personal space, such as colors, patterns, or symbols. Take a moment to sit with your creation and observe your bubble.

Reflections

While observing your work, take a moment to reflect on these questions—feel free to journal your thoughts if it resonates with you.

- How did you feel while creating your bubble?
- Are you satisfied with your bubble and what's inside/outside?
- Are there any changes you would like to make?
- What did you understand about your boundaries through the boundary bubble?

CRAFTING YOUR NARRATIVE

Material Required

- Plain notebook or blank sheets of paper
- Colored markers, pencils, or paints
- Any decorative elements (stickers, washi tape, etc.)

Instructions (Read the story)

The Notebook's New Story

On a dusty shelf in a small bookstore, there sat a notebook. Its cover was plain, its pages crisp and white, waiting to be filled with stories, sketches, or secrets. But day after day, people passed it by, choosing colorful notebooks with glittery covers instead.

The notebook sighed (if a notebook could sigh). "What's wrong with me?" it wondered. "Why won't anyone pick me?"

One evening, just as the bookstore was about to close, a young girl wandered in. She had been looking for the perfect notebook, but nothing seemed quite right. As she walked by the plain notebook, she stopped and picked it up.

"You're not very flashy," she said, flipping through the empty pages, "but I think you'll do."

The notebook felt a flutter of excitement. It was finally chosen! It would finally have a purpose!

Over the next few weeks, the girl filled the notebook with all sorts of things. Poems, doodles, dreams, and worries—all spilled onto the pages. But something was different.

The girl didn't write neatly; she scribbled and scratched, crossing things out, and adding bits of tape and scraps of paper. Sometimes she even dripped paint on the pages.

At first, the notebook was horrified. It wanted to be neat, tidy, perfect! But as the pages filled with the girl's thoughts, the notebook began to see itself in a new light.

Each messy page told a story, not just of the girl's life but of her creativity and imagination. The notebook realized it was more than just a vessel for neat handwriting—it was a companion, a place for the girl to express herself freely without worrying about perfection.

By the time the notebook was full, it was no longer plain or ordinary. It was bursting with life, color, and character. And it was proud to be the notebook that had captured all of the girl's dreams.

Reflections

Take a moment to reflect on these questions—feel free to journal your thoughts if, it resonates with you.

- Create a piece of response art that embodies your personal story of feeling unseen. Use colors, symbols, or images that represent your journey and transformation. What do these elements signify for you?
- How did you feel while reading the story? Did you identify with the notebook in any way?
- What emotions arose for you?
- What does this activity teach you about the value of imperfection in your own life?

STORY IN MOTION

Material Required

- Photos and videos that hold personal significance
- Video editing software or app
- A device to create the video (computer, tablet, or smartphone)
- A journal or notebook for reflection

Instructions

Choose your favorite photos and videos that evoke any thoughts/emotions or are associated with important memories. Create a film/video with the selected media using a video editing app (such as iMovie, Adobe Premiere Rush, or another available tool).

Arrange them in a sequence that tells a story or flows in a way that feels meaningful to you. Choose a piece of music that resonates with the emotions you want to convey or record a voiceover narrating your thoughts and feelings associated with the media.

Set your preferred music or voiceover as the background. It should convey the emotions and thoughts you wish to express. Take time to watch your video. If you feel comfortable, share your film with friends, family, or a support group.

Reflections

While observing your work, take a moment to reflect on these questions —feel free to journal your thoughts, if it resonates with you.

- How did the process of creating the video for you?
- What emotions did you experience while selecting the photos and videos?
- What story or message does your video story convey?
- How do you feel now, after having created and watched your video?
- How do you feel about sharing your video with others?
- What did you learn about yourself through this process?

TWO SIDES OF ME

Material Required

- A3 size sheet of paper
- Scissors and Glue
- Paints (acrylic, watercolors)
- Paintbrushes
- Markers, Oil pastels, Colored pens
- Glitter, beads, and other craft mediums

Template

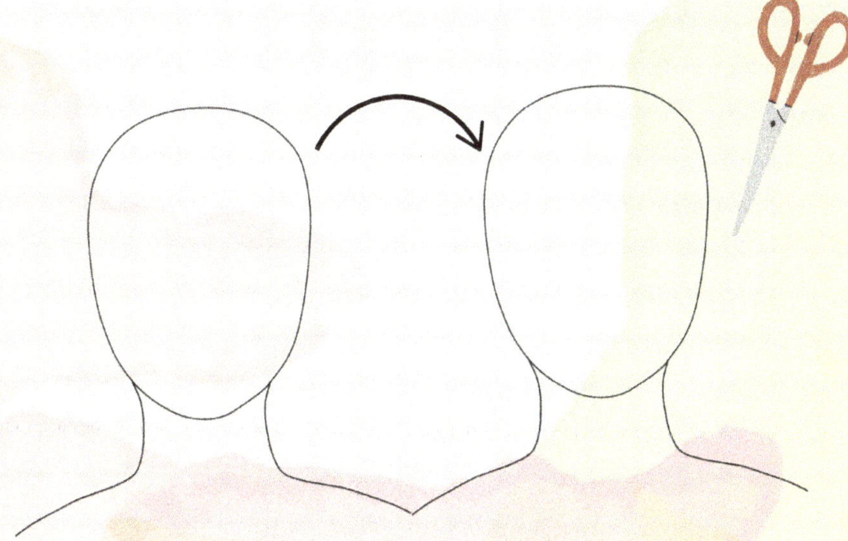

Instructions

Begin by sketching the mask template on your A3 sheet, ensuring it has a comfortable shape with a fold in the center for a greeting card effect. Cut along the outline, leaving the fold intact at the top. Carefully cut out the eye holes as well. Once the mask is cut, open it like a book—one side will represent your inner self and the other your outer self.

Instructions

As you work on the inside of the mask, remember that this area represents your inner self—your feelings, thoughts, ideas, and aspects of your personality that you keep hidden from the world.

Start decorating the inside of the mask using paints, markers, and other craft materials that resonate with your true self. Let your creativity flow and express what's within you.

Once you've completed the inner design, flip the mask over to focus on the outside. This side represents your outer self—the face you present to the world, including the masks you wear in social situations. Choose colors and mediums that symbolize how you want to be perceived.

To add a personal touch, create a greeting or a message that reflects your inner and outer selves. Once both sides of the mask are complete, take a moment to reflect on the differences and similarities between them. What do you notice about your inner and outer selves? How do they connect or diverge?

Reflections

While observing your work, take a moment to reflect on these questions —feel free to journal your thoughts, if it resonates with you.

- How did it feel to create a visual representation of your inner and outer self?
- How does your inner self differ from your outer self as represented on the mask?
- What are the aspects of your inner self that you wish you could show to the outer world?
- Were there any difficulties or surprises that came up for you during mask-making?
- If you want to say something to your inner and outer self, what would it be?

BOX OF HOPE

Material Required

- A plain box (shoebox, wooden box, or any other box)
- Coloured sheets
- Crayons, markers, Paints, and brushes
- Decorative materials (photos, trinkets, stickers, glitter, fabric)
- Paper and pen
- Glue, scissor, and tape

Instructions

Select a box that feels right to you. It can be of any shape and size.

Take a moment to think about hope. What does it mean to you? How would you like to represent your hope in this box?

With this thought decorate your box of hope using different art and craft mediums. Add mediums that symbolize hope for you, such as symbols, words, trinkets, etc.

Once you decorate your box of hope, keep items that inspire you and remind you to stay hopeful in the box. It can be images or souvenirs, or you can also write down your hopes on small pieces of paper and place them inside the box.

You can always come back to this box whenever you need it.

If you feel inspired, create additional boxes for different themes or emotions, such as a Box of Memories, a Box of Joy, or a Box of Strength. Follow the same process.

Reflections

While observing your work, take a moment to reflect on these questions —feel free to journal your thoughts, if it resonates with you.

- What does the concept of hope mean to you, and how did you represent it in your box?
- How did you feel while decorating your box and filling it with hope?
- How do you feel after the process?

IMPRINT IMAGINATION

Material Required

- Aluminum foil
- Acrylic paints
- Paintbrushes or droppers
- A blank sheet of paper (preferably thicker paper or cardstock)
- Palette or mixing tray
- Paper towels or wipes

Instructions

Begin by preparing a piece of aluminum foil; gently crumple it and then flatten it out again to create texture. Using a paintbrush or droppers, apply acrylic paints onto the foil, allowing your creativity to guide you as you scribble or pour the colors. Once you're satisfied with your design, take a blank sheet of thicker paper and carefully place it over the painted foil. Press down gently but firmly to ensure the paint transfers onto the paper. Lift the paper to reveal the beautiful patterns created by your artwork. You can repeat this process with new colors or designs on the same foil to explore further. As your creations dry, take a moment to reflect on the patterns and colors, considering how they resonate with your emotions or experiences.

Reflections

While observing your work, take a moment to reflect on these questions —feel free to journal your thoughts, if it resonates with you.

- What emotions did you feel while creating your piece?
- How do the colors and patterns reflect your current state of mind?
- Did any unexpected shapes or designs emerge during the process? What do they represent for you?
- How can you apply this sense of spontaneity and freedom to other areas of your life?

DOOR OF POSSIBILITIES

Material Required

- Large sheets of paper or cardboard
- Markers, crayons, oil pastels
- Paints (acrylics/ watercolor) and Paintbrushes
- Glue or tape, Scissors
- Various decorative items (magazines for collages, stickers, glitter, fabric scraps, etc.)
- Journal/ Notebook

Instructions

Begin by taking a few moments to think about possibilities and what they mean to you. Think about the opportunities you would like to explore and the goals you have set for yourself.

Then envision a door that leads you to these possibilities. How does the door look? Is it tall or short? What color is it? Is it decorated? Is covered with patterns, or meaningful symbols?

Take a large sheet of paper or cardboard, and draw a door. Consider the shape, size, and design of your door. Is it a simple one, or something unique?

Consider what materials you want to use to design your door. To decorate your door, use markers, colored pencils, or paint. Decorate it with different materials, including details that represent the possibilities you see. Feel free to attach small trinkets or objects that hold value to your door.

Once your door is complete, take a moment to picture opening it. In your journals, describe what you envision beyond the door. It could be a place, a feeling, or a specific scenario that represents the opportunities.

Reflections

While observing your work, take a moment to reflect on these questions—feel free to journal your thoughts, if it resonates with you.

- What does the door symbolize for you?
- What do you see on the other side of the door? What specific opportunities or dreams does your door represent?
- Did you encounter any challenges while creating your door? How did you overcome them?
- What steps you can take in your life to move closer to these possibilities?

SOUNDTRACKS OF LIFE

Material Required

- Paper or a journal
- Colored markers or pencils
- Access to music streaming services (Spotify, Apple Music, etc.)
- Optional: magazine cutouts, stickers, or other decorative items

Instructions

Begin by creating a playlist of songs that hold significance in your life. This could include songs that remind you of important moments, evoke strong emotions, or represent different phases of your journey. Once you have your playlist ready, dedicate a page or section in your journal for each song.

Write down the title, artist, and a brief summary of why this song resonates with you. Use colorful markers or pencils to illustrate your thoughts, incorporating doodles or symbols that represent the feelings each song evokes. You can also add magazine cutouts, stickers, or any other decorative elements that enhance the visual appeal of your pages.

As you work through each song, allow yourself to reflect on the memories or emotions tied to them. Consider how these songs have influenced your experiences and shaped who you are today. By the end of this activity, you will have created a vibrant visual representation of your life's soundtrack.

Reflections

While observing your work, take a moment to reflect on these questions —feel free to journal your thoughts, if it resonates with you.

- What are the thoughts and feelings that emerged during the process?
- Were there any surprises that came up for you? How did it feel to slow down?

JOURNEY MAP

Material Required

- Large sheet of paper or a chart paper
- Colored markers, pens, or pencils
- Paints and brushes
- Stickers, symbols, or small decorative items (optional)
- Glue stick or tape
- Photos (optional)

Instructions

Take a moment to think about the journey you want to map. This could be your current life journey, a specific experience that was significant to you, or your life journey so far.

Consider the major events, emotions, and milestones that impacted your life. Consider what this journey means to you.

Make a mark on your paper to indicate where your journey will begin. This could represent the beginning of the situation or the start of your life journey.

Mark any notable points or incidents that occurred along the way. These can be challenges, achievements, turning points, or moments of change. Use symbols, colors, or pictures to represent each key moment.

As you map out these moments, think about how you felt during each one. Express your emotions using colors, shapes, or phrases. There is no right and wrong; this is your personal journey map.

Add any other details that are important to your journey. This could include people who supported you, obstacles you faced, or lessons you learned. Feel free to add symbols, images, or anything else that reflects your experience. Once your map is complete, take some time to reflect on your journey as a whole.

Reflections

While observing your work, take a moment to reflect on these questions—feel free to journal your thoughts, if it resonates with you.

- What emotions did you experience while creating your journey map?
- What are the most significant moments you included on your map?
- How has your journey shaped who you are today?
- If you were to continue this journey map into the future, what would you hope to see on it?

KEEP THE CREATIVE JUICES FLOWING
CONTINUING YOUR THERAPEUTIC JOURNEY

As you wrap up your exploration of these art therapy techniques, remember that this is just the beginning of your journey. The tools and practices you've experienced have laid a solid foundation, but there are endless opportunities to keep deepening your connection with art as a way of self-expression, reflection, and healing.

Here are a few ways to continue incorporating art into your path of creative growth and discovery:

Make Art a Regular Practice

You can set aside time each day or week to create. It doesn't have to be elaborate — you can maintain a sense of inner connection merely by scribbling or using colors to express yourself. The key is to keep the practice consistent.

Start an Art Journal

You can keep track of your emotional journey by keeping an art journal in which you incorporate drawings with notes or poetry. This will be a private space where you can express your feelings, dreams, and challenges in visual form. Then, reflect on what those expressions reveal about your inner world.

Consider Professional Support

If you ever feel like you want to go deeper into your emotions or address more complex feelings, you can seek out a certified art therapist. They can guide you in a more structured way, helping you explore the parts of yourself that may need professional support.

Create Personal Rituals with Art

You can develop personal rituals that involve art, like monthly check-ins where you create artwork that reflects how you've been feeling or where you are on your journey. Rituals can offer a sense of structure and purpose, keeping you connected to your creative process.

Share your Creations

Sharing art with others can provide support and connection, even though it can be extremely personal. If you feel comfortable doing so, you can opt to share your artwork and open yourself to the experiences and reflections of others, whether it's with close friends, family, or a community.

Join Art Communities

Connecting with people who are traveling a similar path can be immensely fulfilling. Consider participating in art therapy workshops, support groups with Therapy Palette, or somewhere else. These environments foster community, inspire creativity, and offer new perspectives, allowing you to continue learning and growing alongside others.

As you close this book, remember that it marks the beginning of an ongoing journey of creativity and self-discovery. By continuing to explore art therapy, you'll deepen your understanding of yourself, encourage personal growth, and unlock new pathways to emotional healing. The canvas of your life remains wide open, waiting for your next inspired stroke.

WE CAN STAY IN TOUCH!!

Expressive Art Therapy Session at Therapy Palette

At Therapy Palette, my mission is to support you on your journey toward healing, personal growth, and self-reconnection. I am committed to helping you achieve a profound sense of wholeness that enriches every aspect of your life. Our one-on-one sessions are tailored to your unique needs, whether you choose to work with me online or at our studio in Delhi, India. We'll start with an intake call to understand your goals. I am dedicated to guiding you through this transformative process.

One-on-one expressive art therapy at Therapy Palette offers deeper insight and integration, helping you navigate life's challenges and foster personal growth.

Let's keep the conversation going! Connect with me on social media or visit our website to discover how we can continue this journey together.

YOU CAN FIND ME ON

 @therapy_palette

 www.therapypalette.com

**MENTAL HEALTH CLINIC &
ART THERAPY STUDIO**